Best wishes
Harry

Accolades for Potatoes? Not Yet!

"A reflective insight into the power of timing. As a pilot and a business leader, I find Potatoes? Not Yet! a terrific tool to harvest the impact of your team's creative dynamics."

Jorge L. Fernadez, Vice President
International & Alliances, Delta Airlines

"Harry Vardis harvests his own creativity by providing an entertaining and engaging book that will help you explore YOUR creative impulses. Potatoes? Not Yet! breaks down the barriers that inhibit our ability to see our ideas transformed into action."

William Pate, Vice President, Marketing
BellSouth Corporation

"Harry Vardis has crafted an extremely compelling and provocative spring board for anyone looking to expand their creative horizons. Resulting from thousands of hours exploring the underlining dynamics that drive the creative process, Potatoes? Not Yet! is a delightful and unexpected look at the key principals and behaviors that produce this allusive thing we call, creativity. A must read for anyone seeking to create and maintain a working environment of new ideas and progressive thinking."

Steven Gilliatt, President
G2 Worldwide

"This is a highly readable, fun book with enormous potential to get creativity going in you and your company. Once I started reading it, I could not put it down until I finished!"

Jagdish N. Sheth
Charles H. Kellstadt Professor of Marketing
Goizueta Business School, Emory University

"Whether you decide to skim this book or take a deeper dive into each chapter, you'll discover a bounty of ideas that will help you unleash your own personal creativity and spark imagination in others. In either case, absorb and internalize what Potatoes? Not Yet! has to offer. It's a rich harvest of practical recommendations that anyone could easily apply to everyday life."

Bob Kornecki, Midwest Market Leader
Burson-Marsteller

"There is something in this book for everyone. Harry's Greek heritage is showing in the philosophical bent he has couched this treatment of creativity. I enjoyed it, I learned from it and I recommend it to corporate managers and others who want their people to think creatively!"

Walt Lincer,
Vice President of Sales & Marketing
Citrus World, Inc

Potatoes? Not Yet!

33 Ways to Grow & Harvest Your Best Ideas

Harry Vardis

Illustrations by Tony Anthony

Potatoes? Not Yet!
by Harry Vardis

Editor: Sara Kahan
Illustrator: Tony Anthony
Copyright ©2005 Harry Vardis

For more information, contact:
James & Brookfield Publishers
P.O. Box 768024
Roswell, GA 30076

Library of Congress Cataloging in Publication

ISBN: 0-9749191-8-7

10 9 8 7 6 5 4 3 2 1
Printed in the United States of America

The Story Behind the Title

There is a story behind the title of this book.

I was five years old, exploring the neighborhood beyond our house in a suburb of Athens, Greece, when I found Tassos the farmer tending his fields. On his small farm he grew lettuce, tomatoes, onions, parsley, dill, carrots and potatoes. He even grew enough grapes at another location to make his own wine. Great wine according to my father, and totally organic by today's standards.

That day, Tassos stood on top of a flat board behind his horse. He held the reins while the horse pulled the board and an attached hoe that was unearthing potatoes from the ground. When he saw me standing there watching, mesmerized by the sight, he offered: "How would you like to go for a ride?"

"Yes!!!" I almost screamed with excitement at the possibility of a ride with the horse.

He pulled me up on top of the board with him, supported me between his legs, and we started to move. At first, I stood there petrified, looking at the horse's huge rear end right in front of my face and wondering if the horse might kick us both with those powerful legs. Then I relaxed and began to watch the hoe dig deep into the earth, causing potatoes to pop out in all sizes and shapes. It was mystifying to this 5-year-old not only how they got there, but also how Tassos knew they were there.

This was fun! Tassos was singing, the horse was moving calmly, the potatoes were jumping out of the ground, and all was well with my world.

Naturally, I wanted to do this again, so I arrived back at the farm early the next morning. But the potatoes had been harvested and Tassos was off doing other chores. Every day I would come to the farm and ask him "Potatoes?" and his answer was always "Not yet." I would have to wait another whole year.

Many years later, as an adult, I was spending time at a monastery in the holy area of Mount Athos in Northern Greece. One day I asked one of the monks, Father Lucas, the question "How can I make something happen?"

"Be a good farmer," he answered, and walked away.

I followed after him, asking, "Will you please explain to me what that means?"

"A good farmer," he replied, "is one who knows when to put the seed down, when to cultivate it, when to water the soil, and when to harvest. When you have an idea — that is the seed — be sure to take good care of it, to cultivate it well, to bring it out when the time is right. Just like a fruit that is inedible if you cut it before it is ready or that rots on the tree if you leave it there too long, ideas have to be harvested when the time is right."

The title of this book is the product of these two incidents and it is about timing. The book is about cultivating and harvesting your ideas both in your personal and your professional life. Are your potatoes (ideas), which grow underground in your mind, ripe for harvest yet? Do you know how to plant the seeds? Do you know how to care for them? Do you know how to protect them from such pests as idea-killer statements in meetings: "We can't do that," "We tried that and it didn't work," "If you want to get fired try that!"

These poems and tips are an idea-farmer's tools. Use them to help you deal with a challenge, to provide a break in your daily routine or for inspiration. Share them with your friends and co-workers, to let them know that you value their ideas and their thinking.

Be a mindful farmer of your ideas because, just like potatoes, they grow in the far corners of your mind that you cannot see — and they will pop out in all sorts of wondrous sizes and shapes if you use the right tools to nurture and harvest them.

Preface

What you are holding in your hands is a compilation of key principles we, at the Creative Focus Institute, teach MBA and Executive MBA students. I am thrilled to have written this book because it is what the students themselves consider to be the most important things THEY have learned from "The Innovative Leader" course. The principles in this book have helped make a creative difference in their personal lives and career paths.

The Creative Focus Institute has been offering this course for the past six years through business schools at universities as diverse as Emory and Kennesaw in Atlanta, Lake Forest Graduate School of Management in Chicago, and Universidad Anahuac and Novartis University in Mexico City. Students range from recent college graduates to mid- and late-career professionals. They have received the course enthusiastically, with such responses as:

*"Forced me to start thinking outside my comfort zone —
and loving it"*

*"In heated competition, creativity is the differentiator.
Thanks for the armament!"*

"Intense, focused, the best team building experience"

*"It was the most useful course to apply what we learned to
our personal and working life"*

*"This is an amazing course and it sets our school apart
from other graduate programs"*

*"Should be a mandatory core course for all MBA and
EMBA students"*

"Truly a life-changing experience"

Having heard and seen in writing these comments, I became obsessed with the challenge of how to bring these principles to the outside world. How to share them with the people who are not in our classes but who could benefit from knowing and using these principles? This book is something I've wanted to offer ever since I saw the students' reactions and listened to their feedback about what a great learning experience this course had been for them.

Now the time has come to share some of what we teach in these courses with you. You are a manager of your life, your job, your family, your friends and your co-workers. I hope you will find the principles of the stories energizing, intriguing and helpful to producing and harvesting ideas you can use.

In *Potatoes? Not Yet!* I looked at the world of ideas with a Zen-like perspective. The lyrics look deceptively simplistic. Yet, they contain concepts that govern complex thinking.

Enjoy cultivating and harvesting yours and your team's ideas. Your creativity is your ultimate resource. Remember: Your potatoes are waiting to be harvested!

Harry Vardis

Dedication

*Dedicated to my parents Demetrios and Maria Vardis,
my mentor and friend Tassos Vretos,
Father Lucas who lives in the Monastery of Filotheou
in Ayion Oros, and to Sid Parnes,
the man who taught all of us at the
Creative Problem Solving Institute how to think creatively.*

Acknowledgements

Some "Thanks" from the Heart

Everyone we meet has something to teach us. This fact creates a dilemma for me. There is no way I could list everyone who has contributed to the insights that prompted me to write this book. Therefore, I will simply say that I am grateful to all the teachers who shaped my life.

I am particularly grateful to people and institutions who helped to make our courses a huge success and the people who contributed with abundance to make it real:
- The Goizueta Business school at Emory University
- The Michael J. Coles College of Business at Kennesaw State University
- The Lake Forest Graduate School of Management
- The IDEA group at Universidad Anahuac in Mexico City.

I am grateful to Jacquie Lowell for all the editing and encouragement she offered and to Shirley Harris who created the puzzles and for the endless computer hours that it took to put the entire book together.

To the talented art director and good friend, Tony Anthony, who was willing to take a chance on my idea. He created all the wonderful sketches for all of the chapters . . . what better art work could I have asked for?

And finally all my good friends who encouraged me to write the book: David Gonzalez, Mrs. Blanck, Alan Black, Blair Miller, Jack Wolf, Alex Jaccaci, Marcie Seagal, John Peponis and Paul Plsek.

And there is one more person who encouraged me to keep going but who prefers to stay in the background. This is her way of making me a hero. My wife, Athena, who loved the idea from the first moment she read the first poem.

Table of Contents

Chapter 1

The fertile fields of your mind will produce many ideas! Be a good farmer and a good facilitator.

"We know where most of the creativity, the innovation, the stuff that drives productivity lies - in the minds of those closest to the work."

Jack Welch

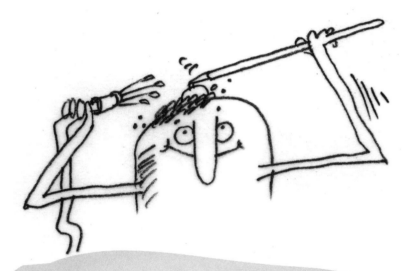

The human mind has been called the ultimate resource. It is a field of all knowledge. It is the hard drive which, when accessed properly, can yield infinite possibilities. To achieve this, we must be aware of our thoughts, find ways to capture them, and nurture them to their fullest potential. We also need to have a process in place and be the facilitators who will allow the process to work.

Live the magic of your mind

Live the magic of your mind
Go as far as you can't reach
And the treasures you will find
Are there . . .. In your golden mind's beach

You have thoughts like precious stones
Tucked in your imagination
They're deep-rooted in your bones
And they are part of your creation

The ideas you can bear
Are for all of us to share
They are yours and yes . . . they're mine
Live the magic of OUR mind!

The multitude of connections that produce our ideas can increase exponentially when we are willing to join mental forces with others. The possibilities for new ideas become endless.

Quantity breeds quality

Ideas appear by surprise it seems
Could be in the shower or perhaps in your dreams
Be ready to capture yours in advance
For once they're gone, there is no second chance

Make lists of them all, go for many
And for sure they're worth
More than a penny

List all yours and those of another
You'll be thankful as you discover
Connect, extend and try to hitchhike
This is no time to close the dike

Make your lists long . . . even longer if you can
At the end of the list you'll understand
You must have many and go far
If you want to discover the right, bright star

Training the brain to come up with many ideas increases the probability to arrive at new and valuable ideas. Try different techniques, e.g., connect, stretch and hitchhike on others' ideas.

Be a facilitator of a creative climate

Be open, be happy
Be fun and be zappy!

Let them know you care to hear 'em
You listen, you smile
You record and stay near 'em

Ask honest questions and help others explore
Take them to exotic travels into their core

Excite them, intrigue them and make them laugh
Help them to see that they have the right stuff

And soon they'll discover the magic voilá
How you change your ideas from "ha-ha" to ah-ha!!

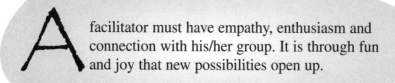

A facilitator must have empathy, enthusiasm and connection with his/her group. It is through fun and joy that new possibilities open up.

Listen generously

My orders are clear, my orders are tall
I came to listen and learn from you all

My motives are pure
My thoughts are sincere
What's in your mind
Is important and dear

I'm here to listen
To ask and explore
Open your mind
And tell me some more

You have all your answers
And yours . . . and yours . . .
We are one team together
Let's sail to new shores

Now take the helm
To lead us ahead
Listen to each other
From your toes to your head

Listen to bodies
Observe how they speak
They give you the clues
To valleys and peaks

As a facilitator your most important task is to listen. Listen with all your senses, not only to what is said, but also observe the body language. It is also important for the participants to listen to each other and build on their ideas.

Smile

It's been said that a smile
Brightens the room
It lifts the spirits and acts like a broom

It sweeps all reservation
And all hesitation
And you can bet that it draws
Everyone's attention

Shower with smiles each one in your team
Let them know you care
And coax them to dream
Imagine and dare
Take risks and go there!

Play with their minds
It's good for their soul
It makes their hearts smile
And pleases them all

A smile is a kiss
To the eyes of your friend
It's the hand he wants you
To warmly extend.

 smiling face wins over a frown all the time. Try making your team's hearts smile!

Use "I wish..." "Wouldn't it be nice...?" "How to...?" and "In what ways might I..."

Use "I wish . . ." to zoom and swish
Turn a problem to a goal
Make it land into your dish
Break big tasks to very small

"Wouldn't it be nice . . ." to add some spice
Get the team to all agree
Focus, dare, list and compare
It is easier when you share

Use "How to . . ." when you diverge
And ideas will emerge
Write them fast change your perspective
Till you find your true objective

If you try "In what ways might I . . ."
You'll be reaching for the sky
Yours are all the possibilities
And they're matched by your abilities

Try twenty or even fifty
Let your list be long and nifty
You will see the real issue...
It is wrapped in fine tissue!

sing these "statements starters" allows you to reframe a challenge and turn it to a wish or a goal. It opens up possibilities for new options. Use the "statement starter" suggestions here to paraphrase your challenge.

Chapter 1 — Learnings

The words to fit in this puzzle can be found throughout the chapter. See how many learnings you have retained.

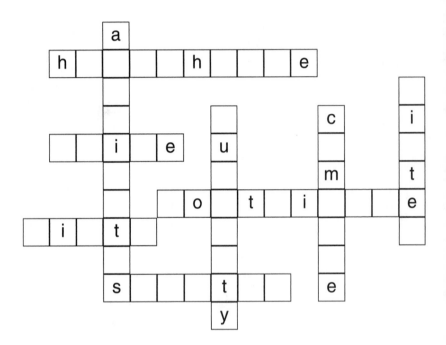

In which three of these principles do you feel you need some improvement?

1._____

2._____

3._____

What will you do differently as a result of what you have learned?

Chapter 2

If you do not bring your ideas to light, they will die

"The cave you fear to enter holds the treasure you seek."

Joseph Campbell

"Most of the important things in the world have been accomplished by people who have kept on trying when there seemed to be no hope at all."

Dale Carnegie

Being brave enough to take risks and looking at failure as a teacher are two critical attributes of creative thinkers. They do not wallow in their failures for they look at them as lessons on something that does not work and move on towards the solution. This type of thinking leads faster to solutions.

Dare to suck big*

Do you dare? Do you dare?
Take the plunge and don't compare
Let your thoughts begin to rise
Don't be afraid or compromise

It is through improvisation
You'll discover innovation
Shoot ideas to create
And that's how you innovate

Think, express and then <u>C</u>reate
Screen your thoughts to <u>B</u>usiness plan
It is time to celebrate
With <u>A</u>pproval from the clan (Top Management, that is)

Dare to risk and dare to try
Dare to whisk and dare to fly
Dare to dig yours is the gig
Most of all dare to suck big!

*Jacquie Lowell

The ABC of innovation is Acceptance by management of a Business idea that is Creative. Daring to take big risks is the beginning of the journey. "Daring to suck big" is a line from improvisational theater, and it is meant to instill courage.

Don't forget to breathe

Take 3 breaths
And say aaaaah!
Pause for breath
Through the blah, blah

Give your brain oxygenation
It deserves a small vacation

Stretch and breathe
You need a break
Help your mind to come awake

Move around and shake on cue
Stretch and bend unblocks your view

If you are facilitating
Give a break without waiting
Every 10 minutes or so
It will help your sessions' flow

B rain breaks are activities designed to energize the body and brain every seven to ten minutes during a presentation or a meeting.

Fail often in order to succeed sooner

Failure's only in your mind
Look ahead and not behind

When you test the possibilities
You're in touch with your abilities

Every time you don't succeed
You know how not to proceed

For it's failure that will guide you
To ideas from inside you

Do it often, plenty of times
Think "how to.." find the enzymes

You'll achieve your true objective
Failing often is subjective

Failing often teaches lessons
Not well known to other persons

"How to" and "How not to"
"What to do" and "What to not do"

As they struggle with duress
Yours will be the big success

Turning failure into a positive and accepting it as a lesson rather than a "failure" helps you accelerate the discovery of the path to the solution that exists at the core of your challenge.

Chapter 2 — Learnings

Find the words in the grid. Pick them out from left to right, top line to bottom line. Words can go horizontally, vertically and diagonally in all eight directions.

ACCEPTANCE	BREATHE	CREATIVE	FAIL OFTEN
BRAIN BREAKS	BUSINESS	DARE	IMPROVISE

```
A F T T Q H R O B U B E Z L F
C C U W R X D B S W R S K U P
V B C R Z Y I B N P A I U T F
X U Y E B C I E H M I V Z S J
V K D C P R W N A Y N O C B H
K G E C U T A H O D B R R X W
J F I Y M Z A Y U F R P E J K
U L K H N K J N G H E M A E H
B U S I N E S S C J A I T H O
F A I L O F T E N E K V I T U
N M G P D S M A P G S H V A S
P K Q L I X L K R H F T E E W
K H I V N C S M H T L V E R U
N G D K G K N R H E F E Q B S
E R A D V T P A S C S O A Z S
```

In which three of these principles do you feel you need some improvement?

1._____

2._____

3._____

What will you do differently as a result of what you have learned?

Chapter 3

Defer Judgment

"There is one thing stronger than all the armies in the world, and that is an idea whose time has come."

Victor Hugo

"A new idea is delicate. It can be killed by a sneer or a yawn; it can be stabbed to death by a quip and worried to death by a frown on the right man's brow."

Charles Brower

The sheer complementation of these two statements demonstrates the essence of this chapter. Judgment is the quickest idea killer and should never be present when ideas are born. It should be kept out of the room until it is time to evaluate ideas. Mistakes are not "wrong acts." They are paths which lead to ideas whose time has not come yet.

Defer judgment of your ideas while you bring them to light

Wise teachers say
"Think before you judge"
Listen carefully
Absorb and nudge

Be sure you have
Criteria in place
And your judging's done
On a solid base

Defer your judgment
When birthing an idea
It is still connected
To your fantasia

It is fragile and needs
Your support to survive
To grow and be strong
Needs your love to stay alive

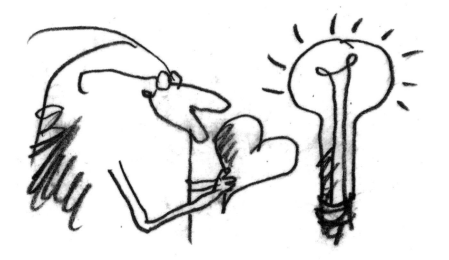

eferring judgment, until all ideas have been listed, helps the idea flow and encourages all ideas to emerge.

Allow yourself 30 mistakes a day

It is human to have some give and take
And in the process you make more than one mistake

You try this and you try that
And you don't know where the solution's at

Mistakes are for people
And people for mistakes
We support each other
And we give what it takes

You want to be right
But you simply can't
When you feel like you're failing
Ask for a hand

So cut yourself slack
Throughout all your days
And make your share of thirty mistakes

By looking at mistakes as teachers, we learn from them and are excited about the possibility to arrive at the right solution soon.

Chapter 3 — Learnings

Find the words in the grid. Words can go horizontally, vertically and diagonally in all eight directions.

CRITERIA   FANTASIA   THIRTY MISTAKES
DEFER JUDGMENT   SUPPORT

```
T T S F N C R I T E R I A B
Q B E K A T R K W G D R R H
N R K L D N M Z W W F F W V
P T A N P E T P G Z Q V J D
J N T K D M C A K L M P F X
J K S N M G M D S D K M X T
Y B I J P D T W X I R K R K
R N M V M U R V K N A O N M
K G Y T W J C C J W P W F F
C T T L M R C V R P B V K G
P N R H R E V R U Q L C C B
R V I F K F Z S R D K Y B R
Z C H W B E B L H R P B T D
Q T T R X D L K H V J Y L L
```

In which three of these principles do you feel you need some improvement?

1._____

2._____

3._____

What will you do differently as a result of what you have learned?

Chapter 4

Are your creative ideas those you like the best?

"What man's mind can create, man's character can control."

Thomas Edison

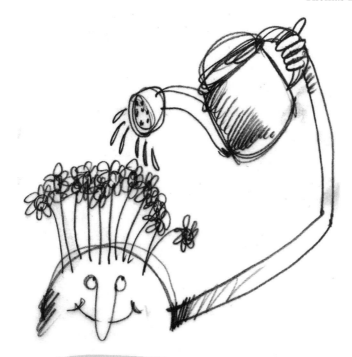

A ttitude and emotional support are very important to the survival of an idea. Our support and the support of others contribute to the genesis and the development of ideas.

Remember to "Yes/And" yourself

Flying in a high altitude
Requires the right attitude

Your ideas are like airplanes
Looking for a place to land
You're the tower to control them
Give them room and put no band

If you do what's always done
You will kill them and they're gone
Prep them right in advance
Give them a survivor's chance

If you use "Yes/ But" to kill
Check your motive and your will
What's behind your objection?
Is it fear of rejection?

Use instead "Yes/ And" support
Give them wings and safe airport
"Yes/ And" builds, supports and grows
Your ideas, and it shows!

N o one kills more of our ideas than we do.
Support and nurture your ideas like a good farmer.

Allow others to support you

Though you like your ideas
And you think they are the best
Let the others to hitch-hike
Bring them on and get some rest

Ask their pluses
Ask their praise
Whether big or small, embrace
It's their thinking that you want
Get the team to play and bond

Being alone in ideation
Gives no room for new creation
It is boring and trite
And your stars won't look so bright

Let them give support to you
Let them build on what is new
Let your thoughts emerge and shine
Let your team do more than nine

Your ideas will flow brighter
And for sure theirs will be lighter
If they give support to you
'Cause they're a big part of your crew

In addition to your support, your ideas need the support of others. Accept it, embrace it and honor it.

Chapter 4 — Learnings

Find the words in the grid. Pick them out from left to right, top line to bottom line. Words can go horizontally, vertically and diagonally in all eight directions.

ALLOW	IDEAS	SUPPORT
EMBRACE	NURTURE	TEAM
FEAR	RISK	YES

```
S U E R U T R U N T
P P O E R T R A N R
D N U R M I T D U O
F E A R S B N R W P
S E Y K O A R O U P
T A R I D E L A A U
E S E L I L K E C S
A A G D A O S O D E
M F A R I M E E R L
L W Z X L T Y N P N
```

In which three of these principles do you feel you need some improvement?

1._____

2._____

3._____

What will you do differently as a result of what you have learned?

Chapter 5

Remember to praise the ideas of others before you judge them

"The beginning of wisdom is the definition of terms."

Socrates

By first praising an idea we encourage it to grow. Also, we encourage the birth of others.

Praise first

"The cosmos begins in our eyes
and ends in our dreams"
this embraces all, or so it seems

There are protons and neutrons
And particles of matter
We don't even know
And what keeps them together
Is hard to show

Is it magic or glue
From the Universe of stars
Or maybe the music
From some God's guitars

Is it something we're born with
And we all do possess?
Is it our power to smile
When others caress?

Yes, it's in us
It's big, and its beauty is real
It's the praise we receive
and we know how we feel

Praise first, hold rejection for later
'cause the praise you give
makes a man a creator

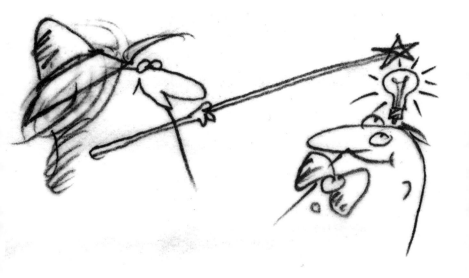

Praise is the warmest and most powerful way to reinforce others' ideas. Give it with abundance.

Support and build on others' ideas

Start with "In what ways might I . . ."
Then magnify and rearrange
Throw all objections to the sky
'Cause everything's within your range

Ride on everyone's ideas
Step out of your box
Dare to dream, adapt, reverse
Free-wheel and be a fox

Imagine, match, associate
Isn't it fun to ideate?

Force new relations and find new potions
Use many analogies and lists
Give your support to other's notions
Go for different twists

Be in an African Safari
Glide the Alps or fly in space
Think you're an Indian with a sari
And keep a smile on your face

Take your thoughts that seem so strange
Twist and turn and twist again
Make them small, big, rearrange
Then load them in a brand new train

S upport the ideas of others. Go on mind excursions. Be playful and the result is always a big surprise!

Use criteria when you judge

I have often thought that criteria are like bacteria;
When they are attached to ideas they survive,
When they are not, they die.

An idea on its own has no legs to stand
And it needs the support of a valuable friend

May need "money," may need "time"
Or may need people with passion
These criteria will determine the amount of compassion

For the life of a thought
Can be seriously at stake
If there are no criteria
To evaluate

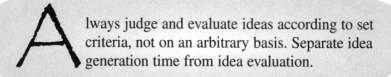

lways judge and evaluate ideas according to set criteria, not on an arbitrary basis. Separate idea generation time from idea evaluation.

Chapter 5 . . . Learnings

Find the words in the grid. Pick them out from left to right, top line to bottom line. Words can go horizontally, vertically and diagonally in all eight directions.

JUDGE   FIRST   EMBRACE   EVALUATE
PRAISE   REINFORCE   CRITERIA

```
E E Z S F Y R P S U P E Y I B
U V N N A M R X D G C S T K E
B S A W X A E L P R Q S Z Y C
H E T L I M J D O E G D U J J
I M W S U Q Z F D N P R W I N
Z B E U D A N C R I T E R I A
O R Y A O I T H C W Z V Z Y S
O A D O E X H E B S W I P M U
Y C S R I Q K M W X J U U T H
W E D K O P Q W G L T P T Q J
Q K U E A G F W D R E S Q B O
W S Q S B R Q C U A G O R Q V
S R A W I W R V P X H U U I I
G C M R H H P H G I X V D F F
R B Y U I L C O S P Z C Q L W
```

In which three of these principles do you feel you need some improvement?

1._____

2._____

3._____

What will you do differently as a result of what you have learned?

Chapter 6

What ideas would you bring out if you weren't afraid?

"Don't let your fears stand in the way of your dreams."

Anonymous

"One cannot always be a hero, but one can always be a human."

Goethe

*"First they ignore you.
Then they laugh at you.
Then they fight you.
Then you win. "*

Gandhi

Courage, determination and perseverance are the paths to finding solutions. Solutions are ideas that fit the criteria necessary to reach a goal. Positive support through the creative process is the mortar that keeps the structure together and produces positive and rich results.

Judge affirmatively

What will they think
What will they say
What would you do
If you could have your way?

If fear is the king
That dictates behavior
You'll feel the sting
That carries no favor

You hold back your thoughts
You squash your idea
They think you're a whoosh
With no fantasia

Now move on ahead
Use praise right up front
It is best to judge
Holding back the "won't"

See the pluses first
In someone else's thoughts
Give support and burst
Leave the juggernauts

Fear of failure makes us hold back our ideas. By first praising the ideas of others, we encourage them, and they encourage us in turn to bring new ideas to life.

Support your team as a leader

To know yourself you will agree
It takes courage and it is key
You want to guide
your team through adventures
To come out winners
in all new ventures

Your manners, your zings,
your words and your attitude
Will give them wings
and lots of latitude

They'll love to explore
to search and do more
hold them close to your chest
show them trust and have zest

Be a leader who cares
And one who dares
Listen, observe and show reverence
The people you lead
Will want to succeed
As long as your guidance shows relevance

A leader's role is to induce new ideas. A good leader guides and supports his team through all challenges. Positive attitude is the first and foremost key ingredient to motivate your team to generate new ideas.

Chapter 6 — Learnings

Find the words in the grid. Words can go horizontally, vertically and diagonally in all eight directions.

PLUSES	REVERSE	COURAGE	CARING
CONCERNS	COMBINE	ATTRIBUTES	OBSERVE

```
G T J S F Q G V Y S L H O M V
C N K K E D H U V E X C I Q K
B H I S X V S L S T N I T Q F
Z T H R M C A R H U Q K M H A
Q W X S A C I S J B I O A F E
F C A S M C N X H I E O Q I M
R L O S D R L G F R H L F C U
F X I M E G O W Z T Z V X O Z
D E P C B B X O O T M H J U I
V D N R S I P Q L A T G P R D
D O A E T P N I B X J L Q A R
C V R F B L R E I V Y V X G F
W V M G T P I X N N I W Z E I
E K D S T Q M S E S U L P Y H
R E V E R S E J M R M A R P I
```

In which three of these principles do you feel you need some improvement?

1._____

2._____

3._____

What will you do differently as a result of what you have learned?

Chapter 7

Use many and different seeds to cross-fertilize new ideas

"If a man does not keep pace with his companions, perhaps it is because he hears a different drummer."

Henry David Thoreau

"Do not follow where the path may lead. Go instead where there is no path and leave a trail."

Ralph Waldo Emerson

Diverge, Converge and be happy

Open up and thoughts will flow
Write them down and they will grow

Pop them up and fill the easel
Don't be afraid of the weasel

Hold your judgment in the back
Just defer it, don't get stuck!

Go for more and more potatoes
They don't bite like alligators

Fill the bucket with them all
Build on others, go for more

Stretch and seek for wild and funny
In the hat there is a bunny!

When converging to criteria
Treat them not like bad bacteria

For behind every invention
There's a positive intention

Be deliberate and thoughtful
Don't be harsh,
Be smart and watchful

Check the objectives
Judge with vision
To arrive at your decision

Build on those that need new legs
Even if they're wooden pegs

Go for new and brave potatoes
Don't get stuck with dried tomatoes

Pick the brand new and the bold
They're the ones that hide the gold!

Diverge first on new ideas and follow with convergence to the select few that meet the criteria. Keep an open mind so that ideas will flow. An open mind celebrates the birth of new ideas.

Ask "What" questions

Start your questions with a "What"
And response will vary a lot

Ask for 3 or 4 things to list
And you get into the gist

What are 3 foods that you like?
What are 3 things that you need?
What 3 cars do look alike?
What are 3 books that you read?

"What" explores the inner feelings
Lets you see and feel and think
You discover inner meanings
"What's" the chisel to dig deep

What 3 hobbies that you like can tell me?
What 3 movies do you like?
What are 3 things you can sell me?
What 3 treks you like to hike?

You can gather information
With a "What" in just a jiffy
For success and innovation
"What" is very, very spiffy!

sk questions that start with "What" and demand a number of answers, e.g. "What 3 . . ." or "What 5 . . .." This type of phrasing opens up possibilities for a variety of ideas to emerge on any subject.

Change perspectives

For ideas with notoriety
You must try some variety

Break down present assumptions
And forget all your presumptions

Join the best of the photographers
learn some lessons from cartographers

They do change their perspectives
Mix and match to their objectives

Change their lenses and their angle
Loose their strings and let them dangle

Mix the colors and the texture
Get a whole new architecture

Change perspectives to your challenge
And you'll drink from a new chalice

Give new eyes to your mind
Go explore and you will find

A new way to a golden nugget
Find solutions right on target!

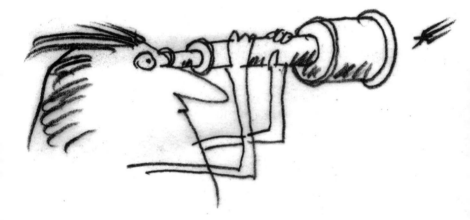

Zoom in and zoom out your lenses to see new possibilities. By changing perspectives you can discover new ways to reframe a challenge. This process allows for new and unexpected solutions.

Take time out to reflect, incubate and rejuvenate

You work all your life from 9 to 5
You study, you practice, you slave and you thrive

Your days are full with no time to play
You meet many people with not much to say

Your living's demanding, your chores are so daunting
And what's left over is not much for flaunting

Your mind is full of thoughts and creativity
But what's really missing is the right activity

You need to take time to think and reflect
To give your ideas a chance to collect

Find a place that's peaceful and right
And let imagination go on its own flight

Allow incubation to take over your brain
And give a vacation to your thought and its train

Remember to breath and oxygenate
As all your ideas will gather and mate

Ideas are like rabbits, you gather a few
Reflect, incubate and there will be a slew

S low down your pace to incubate. Rearrange your thoughts to give new ideas a chance to bubble up.

Chapter 7 — Learnings

Unscramble the tiles to reveal a message from this chapter. Blank spaces indicate the end or beginning of a word.

I V E	VER	SCO	OU	HAL	AYS	DI	RSP
S S	RE	A C	TO	CAN	CHA	G E!	LEN
NGE	NE	W W	ECT	O Y	FRA	P E	ME

In which three of these principles do you feel you need some improvement?

1._____

2._____

3._____

What will you do differently as a result of what you have learned?

Chapter 8

Test the environment for acceptance

"Everyone has a talent; but rare is the courage to follow the talent to the place it leads."

Erica Jong

Taking time to reflect and consider different points of view allows for acceptance of all.

Pause, reflect, respond

Take 10 seconds to respond
To reflect, react and bond
Give 10 seconds to apprise
Wait, be patient, energize

Take some time for reflection
"Pause" is good before objection
Put your thoughts through third degree
If your first thought is "Disagree"

Pause, reflect, respond and praise
Think again and rearrange
All your thoughts that lead to action
Don't rely on first reaction

Give your mind a chance to think
Give your heart a chance to sync
Don't be a jailer of your heart
Hit bull's eye with your dart!

Often, when we don't like someone's idea we don't take time to praise it first. It is better to praise first. Next, take time to pause, and finally, phrase any concerns in the form of "In what ways might we . . ." to overcome the concern.

Respect individual differences — make them your friend and ally

No two grains of sand are ever alike
No two snowflakes were ever the same
No two water drops going through the dike
No two people could be of one flame

Conditions do change
And there are inferences
Our words account
For our personal differences

Each human does grow in this or that way
And has a defined and unique DNA

We may look alike but given our realities
We all have uniquely defined personalities

Religions aside and points of view
We all share the same long queue

It starts with our human condition in mind
And begs for right treatment mostly in kind

We all are governed by the golden rule
The "do unto others . . ." and be no fool

Our differences are human and never so big
That if we walk together we won't succeed

Put aside your ego and share your strength
The road will be easier, you won't know the length

Recognizing individual differences and ideas, accepting them, respecting them and adopting them allows us to bond together at the emotional level.

Chapter 8 — Learnings

Unscramble the tiles to reveal words from this chapter. A '_' designates the end of a word.

_DI	D_B	REN	PAU	NDI	FFE	SE_
ULL	RES	CES	E_I	VID	PON	SEY
UAL

In which three of these principles do you feel you need some improvement?

1._____

2._____

3._____

What will you do differently as a result of what you have learned?

Chapter 9

Imagine how to implement an idea and that will lead you to the solution

"Happiness is when what you think, what you say, and what you do are in harmony."

Mahatma Gandhi

"You must be the change you wish to see in the world."

Mahatma Gandhi

When we are "in the groove" there is perfect harmony and balance.

"Be, Do, Have" is the natural way of life...you can hurt yourself if you reverse it

Take a good look at a clear night sky
And look for a distant and bright golden star

Pray and ask for your thoughts to go fly
To come back and to tell who you are

Discover your talents, your wishes and goal
Bring 'em all forward from the depths of your soul

To know yourself and what will you be
Ask for the Universe and you to agree

Then do what you must to reach your potentials
Reach for that star with all your credentials

Do what it takes and do proceed
If you are who you "is" you will succeed

Only then as a great star you'll possess
The brightness, the glory and all the success

Don't go looking to reverse this law
You'll fail badly because it is natural, you know

We humans forget that to have, do and be
Is reverse to the Universe's law, don't you see?

Dressing like an athlete does not make one an athlete. Be an athlete, do what athletes do and you will have what athletes have. The solutions lie within you.

Mindmapping for fun and profit

The yellow brick road may lead you to Oz
Where wizards and magic, miracles cause

Your Oz is there between your ears
The magic will happen, leave behind your fears

By exploring and mapping the ideas abound
Put the goal in the middle, the paths all around

Give your tree many branches and more branches still
Put the lines in order and color at will

Follow logic, have fun, make it look like a map
Give it names, direction and be sure there's no gap

Plan your day, your trip, your school notes or vacation
Use your pencil, your crayons and your imagination

Teach your children to do it in small easy steps
Teach them logic, correction and thinking that helps

Do diverge and converge using mindmapping now
And the rest will follow, you will see how

It's a tool you can use on ideas to diverge
To create new thoughts and it helps to converge

Mindmapping is a logical way to proceed
When you want all your plans put in place to succeed!

M indmapping is a technique that allows us to create visual representations of ideas and their mutual relationships. It is a blueprint towards solutions. For complete instructions on how to use it see: The Mindmapping Tool based on the mindmapping technique by Tony Buzan.

Embrace enthusiasm and joy!!!!

Do you remember when you got a new toy
The feelings of laughter, excitement and joy?

Remember as you first looked at the box
How you got so sneaky . . . just like a fox?

Curiosity, wonder and anticipation
Teases, excites, alerts the imagination

Unwrap the box, open it up . . . and voilá
The fun has started and it takes you to aha!

Think of your mind in a similar way
A gift box with boxes just hidden away

A life full of gifts to enjoy and open up
To always be surprised at a million aha!

Open them up as often as you like
It's Christmas always, enjoy the red bike

Be enthused, proclaim your gifts and enjoy
Have fun, imagine and embrace a new toy

It is contagious so spread it all around
Your brand new ideas will so magically abound

Enthusiasm sparks the flame of your heart to sparkle and glow
Turns new ideas into rivers that towards you will flow

Enthusiasm brightens and glows on all of your team's faces
Turns skeptics and "yes, but's" always into aces!

E nthusiasm helps to make an ideation session success-
ful. Enthusiasm in your everyday life is contagious
to others and makes for a happier life.

Chapter 9 — Learnings

The words to fit in this puzzle can be found throughout chapter nine. See how many learnings you have retained.

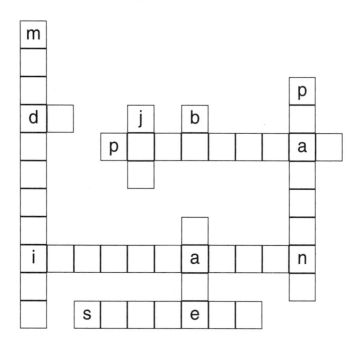

In which three of these principles do you feel you need some improvement?

1._____

2._____

3._____

What will you do differently as a result of what you have learned?

Chapter 10

The sooner you get over your habits, the sooner you will discover new ideas

"People are disturbed not by things but by the view they take of them."
Epictetus, c 200AD

"Whether you believe you can or cannot do something, you are right."
Henry Ford

Every moment of our life can become a new exciting experience if we are willing to make a 10% change in our behavior.

Use the: "Up to now"..."From now on"

Magic words are all around
Fill the minds and abound
Help define and proclaim
Most of all they do reframe

Words like "great" or "wish" or "beauty"
Can be real or sometimes snooty

But what happens when your boss
Makes you feel like real loss?
Problems start and you realize
That you have to compromise
Need reframing not a rub
To move on and save the job

Try reframe with "up to now"
As the words will do their magic
Use them, change the problem's logic
Close the sentence with a vow

Don't know why we disagree, "up to now"
Don't know what he wants of me, "up to now"
Don't know how to go about it, "up to now"
Don't know when to work around it, "up to now"

"Up to now" is uplifting and allows
To reframe, change perspectives, raise some brows

It allows to make a promise to yourself
"Put a stop," "Change your ideas," "look ahead"

"Up to now" by itself is oh!! So lonely
Needs a mate to move along and start the action
"From now on" can make the change and not only
Start the fire for a positive reaction

"From now on" paints a whole new bright picture
Of a promise you can make to yourself
It'll be written right now and in the scripture
That the promise won't be left back on the shelf

To reframe concerns and change circumstances, use "Up to now" to describe what has been going on and "From now on" to proclaim what you will do in the future.

Chapter 10 — Learnings

The words to fit in this puzzle can be found throughout chapter ten. See how many learnings you have retained.

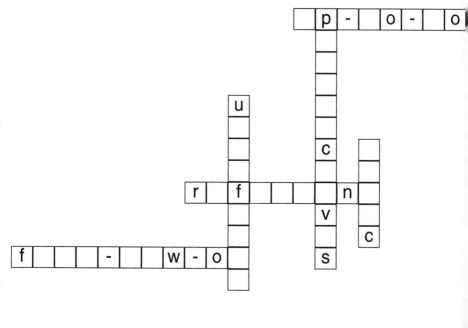

In which three of these principles do you feel you need some improvement?

1._____

2._____

3._____

What will you do differently as a result of what you have learned?

Chapter 11

Auto-pilot patterns do not lead to new ideas

"Innovators and creators are persons who can to a higher degree than average accept the condition of aloneness. They are more willing to follow their own vision, even when it takes them far from the mainland of the human community. Unexplored places do not frighten them — or not, at any rate, as much as they frighten those around them. This is one of the secrets of their power. That which we call 'genius' has a great deal to do with courage and daring, a great deal to do with nerve."

Nathaniel Branden

"Life is not measured by the number of breaths we take, but by the moments that take our breath away."

George Carlin

Change at least one thing you do habitually each day and you will have a new day.

Be playful and wonder...
live your life again!

If I could live my life again
I wouldn't say as many "should's" or "must's"
Nor any "have to's" or "ought to's"

If I could live my life again
I would buy scores of music and words of songs
I would buy poems and children's books not adult "how to's"

If I could live my life again
I'd spend more hours by the water front and under the trees
I'd ask for their wisdom and their knowledge
Not for their warmth in the fire place where they burn like logs
For they have seen so much just by being there
Quietly keeping all their little secrets of the world

If I could live my life again
I wouldn't be impatient about love
For love takes time to find, to grow, to give.
Love spreads like wildfire around you when you feel it
It's not possessive and it does move mountains.
Love also grows mysteriously—sometimes with a word,
Sometimes with a touch and sometimes with a smile.

If I could live my life again
I'd sing to people and talk in the shower
Instead of the other way around.

I'd tell my enemies how important they are to me
For they teach me lots of lessons
And I'd ask my friends how not to spoil me.

I'd tell all the children that they are mine
Because they are part of me
And I'd make sure that everyone knows
The game of life is about sharing not about keeping.

I'd go to places where no one else wants to go to see why they don't—
I'd cry more often in weddings and laugh in funerals
Because that's the way of the fools.

I'd be foolish more often so that people could reach me more—
I'd learn 10 languages but not of people—
I'd speak cat, dog, fish, snake and other animal languages
So that I could hear their pleas—
And I'd be more open to their ideas about the world.
I'd have only one shoe to know what the earth feels
Like under my foot
And I'd tell everyone I love them so that I'd know if I should.

If I could live my life again
"Sadness" would be forbidden
And I would smile when I saw people cry
For I have never seen a rainy day that wasn't followed by sunshine.

If I could live my life again
I'd confess all my good deeds and not my sins
Because God who is in all of us knows best
And our acts are his

If I could live my life again
For sure it wouldn't be in vain!

To enjoy the creative life, step outside the box and experience life from that unusual perspective.

Be spontaneous
to overcome your artist's block

What is a sculptor's knife like?
What is the magic of a moonbeam?
What brings a stone or glass to life?
What makes a painting a dream?

The white canvas is infinity
Challenge and goal to imagination
A rock will challenge your ability
To bring alive your aspiration

Your mind will wander staring at
The white paper off the bat
Might be upset and bit frustrated
Because your thoughts seem so unrelated

You have a vision and a goal
But nothing seems to touch your soul
You need some time to think and ponder
So let your mind play and wander

Start with your body and your toys
It takes first will and then a choice
Play and wander it's your nature
Allow improper nomenclature

Select, reverse, choose, rearrange
Be sure that everything will change

To fill the board with inspiration
First exercise the imagination

To carve the stone to a statue still
Confront your fears, employ your will

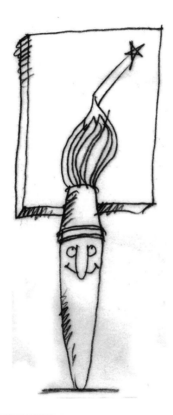

Everybody has an artistic talent. To overcome artist's block and express your artistic abilities you must discover the activities which help you be yourself.

Chapter 11 — Learnings

Unscramble the tiles to reveal words from this chapter. A '_' designates the end of a word.

RAN	NGE	E_R	PLA	ECT	OOS	EAR
CHA	_CH	RSH	DVE	RE_	_LE	GE_
IP_	L_A	NTU	ADE	SEL	YFU	

In which three of these principles do you feel you need some improvement?

1._____

2._____

3._____

What will you do differently as a result of what you have learned?

Chapter 12

Start small and use the right tools

"A will finds a way."

Orison Swett Marden

"An avalanche begins with a snowflake."

Joseph Compton

"An idea is salvation by imagination."

Frank Lloyd Wright

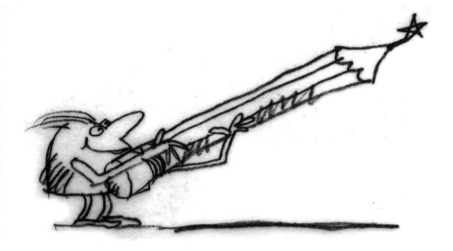

 n easel, Post-It Notes,™ pads, colorful loose sheets of paper are basic tools to an ideation journey.

Use Post Its™ it is a new beginning!

To be a good farmer
And keep the idea flow
Start in small steps
A wish and a glow

Our daily routines
Don't demand creativity
It's the exceptions that call for
And demand such activity

We have to start small and build to new heights
We must start walking before taking long flights

Start small, write them down
Stick Post Its™ all around

Do one on each post it
Use the easel to coast it!

Each idea has a place
And deserves a fair race

Let it fight and compete
Use the Post Its™, don't cheat

Post Its™ help to record
Move around and to board

Cluster them where you must
Your ideas won't be dust

Post Its™ help in ideation
Make a breeze the collation

They will help you succeed
They won't fail, they are the seed.

Post Its™ in many colors excite the imagination and help with the management of the ideation session.

Chapter 12 — Learnings

Unscramble the tiles to reveal a message. Blank spaces indicate the end or beginning of a word.

STA	RIG	E T	LL	RT	HT	TOO
HE	SMA	LS!	US	AND		

In which three of these principles do you feel you need some improvement?

1._____

2._____

3._____

What will you do differently as a result of what you have learned?

Live up to your maximum potential

Cultivate your ideas and they will grow . . . your "gold mind" will produce them

Record your ideas . . . anticipate them and save them

Enhance idea generation using many stimuli to generate ideas . . . Natural phenomena can be the best stimulators for idea generation

Adopt the habit of ideating often . . . Get your mind in the habit of producing lots of ideas

Trust and receive your ideas with enthusiasm . . . Enthusiasm is the single most powerful idea generator

Identify criteria for evaluation when the time is right . . . Have acceptance criteria in place but do not evaluate the ideas while they are born

Vigilance is the mother of new ideas . . . Even when you sleep! When they come, they come in bunches and you must be ready to keep them or lose them

Enjoy and have fun ideating

Epilogue

After completing the reading of this book, I felt the strings of my mental instrument vibrate at frequencies that produced sounds I had never heard before. It seemed that some latent sites of my personality had been activated, and I began to have a better understanding of myself as well as others.

Ambition and creativity go hand-in-hand. Human progress is due to the creative thinking that leads to new ideas that can be realized, that can fulfill some need. A creative person might generate a great number of good ideas, but the number of those that can be realized is limited by time and other constraints.

Realization of ideas or achievement of goals is a time consuming process compared to how rapidly a creative mind generates good ideas. This means that as time passes by there is an ever-increasing "gap" between achieved goals and those in mind. Do not focus on the "gap" but rather on your achievements.

If manifestation of our personality is the feelings and the ideas we express and the manner in which these are communicated to and received by others, then by reading this book, I feel that I have improved myself, I have become a better person.

Constantine Screttas
Research Director
National Hellenic Research Foundation

Puzzle Answers

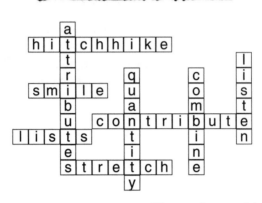

Chapter 1, page 24

Chapter 2, page 32

Chapter 3, page 38

Chapter 4, page 44

Chapter 5, page 52

Chapter 6, page 58

Chapter 7, page 68

"Change perspectives so you can discover new ways to reframe a challenge."

Chapter 8, page 74

Pause, Respond, Bullseye, Individual, Differences

Chapter 10, page 86

Chapter 9, page 82

Chapter 11, page 94

Playful, Adventure, Change, Leadership, Select, Choose, Rearrange

Chapter 12, page 98

Start small and use the right tools!

Bibliography

Black, R.A. PhD. *Broken Crayons*. Dubuque, Iowa: Kendall/Hunt Publishing Company, 1995

Buzan, T. *Use Both Sides of Your Brain*. New York: Dutton, 1976

Daskalopoulos, Demetrios. *Anthology of Poems*. Athens, Greece, 1998

Gonzalez, David. *Begin Within: You Are What You Think*. Book Surge Llc, 2004

Gordon, W.J.J. *Synectics*. New York: Harper & Row, 1961

Higgins, J.M. *101 Creative Problem Solving Techniques*. Winter Park, FL: New Management Publishing Company, Inc., 1994

Lowell, Jacquie.www.jacquielowell.com

Miller, B., Vehar, J., Firestein, R. *Creativity Unbound*. Evanston, IL: THinc Communications, 2003

Parnes, S.J. *A Facilitating Style of Leadership*. Buffalo, NY: The Creative Education Foundation, 1985

Parnes, S.J. *Optimize the Magic of Your Mind*. Buffalo, NY: The Creative Education Foundation, 1997

Plsek, P.E. *Creativity, Innovation and Quality*. Milwaukee, WI: American Society for Quality, 1997

Segal, M. *Creativity and Personality Type*. Huntington Beach, CA: Telos Publications, 2001

Van Gundy, A.B. *Brainboosters for Business Advantage*. San Diego, CA: Pfeiffer and Company, 1995

Wolf, J. PhD. *Powerful Presentation Techniques*. Bradenton, FL: Lifelong Learning Partners, 2003

An IDEA-L book for anyone who manages people and ideas at work, at play, or just in life!

Potatoes? Not Yet!

33 Ways to Grow & Harvest Your Best Ideas

Harry Vardis
Illustrations by Tony Anthony

Order Form

To order *Potatoes? Not Yet!* by phone:
Creative Focus, Inc. 404.256.7000

For creativity and innovation training workshops
call 404.256.7000 or visit www.creativefocus.net
to learn more.

For special quantity discounts, bulk purchases, sales promotions, premiums,
fundraising, or educational use call 404.256.7000 and ask for details.

Mail your order to:
Potatoes? Not Yet!
Creative Focus, Inc.
P. O. Box 501206
Atlanta, GA 31150

Book total:	_____
7% GA sales tax:	_____
Postage & handling:	_____
Total due:	_____

Enclose a check or money order made payable to Creative Focus, Inc.
and allow up to 4-6 weeks for U.S. delivery. Canada or International orders
please allow 6-8 weeks.

Shipping/postage & handling: U.S./Canada $2.75 for one book, $1.00 for
each additional book not to exceed $10.75; International $5.00 for one book,
$1.00 for each additional book.

Please ship [quantity] _____ books to:

_____

Name/Company

_____

Address 1

_____

Address 2

_____

City/State/Zip

_____

E-mail and Phone [for questions regarding order]

To order by credit card or for faster ordering please visit our website at
www.creativefocus.net and click on the *Potatoes? Not Yet!* icon.